LETTERS FROM A FATHER,
AND OTHER POEMS

BOOKS BY MONA VAN DUYN

LETTERS FROM
A FATHER
AND OTHER POEMS

Mona Van Duyn

ATHENEUM   *New York*

1982

POEMS IN THESE PAGES HAVE APPEARED IN:

Poetry: "The Case of The," "The Ballad of Blossom," "Photographs"
The New Yorker: "At Père Lachaise," "Moose in the Morning, Northern Maine"
Ploughshares: "Speak, Memory," "Madrid, May, 1977," "Goya's 'Two Old People Eating Soup'"
Poetry Now: "Letters from a Father" (This poem was reprinted in *Ploughshares* and in *The Pushcart Prize IV*)
The Pomegranate Press: "In the Missouri Ozarks"
The Georgia Review: "Madrid, 1974," "Lives of the Poets," "Fall"
The Little Magazine: "Caring for Surfaces"
American Poetry Review: "Ringling Brothers, Barnum and Bailey"
Crosscountry: "A Reading of Rex Stout"
Counter/Measures: "A Winter's Tale, by a Wife"
The Massachusetts Review: "Saleswomen in Bakery Shops," "The Vision Test"
St. Louis Literary Supplement: "Cinderella's Story"
Michigan Quarterly Review: "The Stream"
The Yale Review: "The Learners"
River Styx: "The Hermit of Hudson Pond"

Library of Congress Cataloging in Publication Data

Van Duyn, Mona.
     Letters from a father, and other poems.

     I. Title.
PS3543.A563L4   811'.54   81-70060
ISBN 0-689-11286-6   AACR2
ISBN 0-689-11287-4 (pbk.)

Published simultaneously in Canada by McClelland and Stewart Ltd
Manufactured by American Book-Stratford Press, Saddle Brook, New Jersey
Designed by Kathleen Carey
First Edition

FOR MY PARENTS

Earl G. Van Duyn 1891–1980

Lora G. Van Duyn 1895–1980

CONTENTS

LAST

LETTERS FROM A FATHER

I

Ulcerated tooth keeps me awake, there is
such pain, would have to go to the hospital to have
it pulled or would bleed to death from the blood thinners,
but can't leave Mother, she falls and forgets her salve
and her tranquilizers, her ankles swell so and her bowels
are so bad, she almost had a stoppage and sometimes
what she passes is green as grass. There are big holes
in my thigh where my leg brace buckles the size of dimes.
My head pounds from the high pressure. It is awful
not to be able to get out, and I fell in the bathroom
and the girl could hardly get me up at all.
Sure thought my back was broken, it will be next time.
Prostate is bad and heart has given out,
feel bloated after supper. Have made my peace
because am just plain done for and have no doubt
that the Lord will come any day with my release.
You say you enjoy your feeder, I don't see why
you want to spend good money on grain for birds
and you say you have a hundred sparrows, I'd buy
poison and get rid of their diseases and turds.

II

We enjoyed your visit, it was nice of you to bring
the feeder but a terrible waste of your money
for that big bag of feed since we won't be living
more than a few weeks longer. We can see
them good from where we sit, big ones and little ones
but you know when I farmed I used to like to hunt
and we had many a good meal from pigeons
and quail and pheasant but these birds won't
be good for nothing and are dirty to have so near
the house. Mother likes the redbirds though.
My bad knee is so sore and I can't hardly hear
and Mother says she is hoarse from yelling but I know
it's too late for a hearing aid. I belch up all the time

and have a sour mouth and of course with my heart
it's no use to go to a doctor. Mother is the same.
Has a scab she thinks is going to turn to a wart.

I I I

The birds are eating and fighting, Ha! Ha! All shapes
and colors and sizes coming out of our woods
but we don't know what they are. Your Mother hopes
you can send us a kind of book that tells about birds.
There is one the folks called snowbirds, they eat on the ground,
we had the girl sprinkle extra there, but say,
they eat something awful. I sent the girl to town
to buy some more feed, she had to go anyway.

I V

Almost called you on the telephone
but it costs so much to call thought better write.
Say, the funniest thing is happening, one
day we had so many birds and they fight
and get excited at their feed you know
and it's really something to watch and two or three
flew right at us and crashed into our window
and bang, poor little things knocked themselves silly.
They come to after while on the ground and flew away.
And they been doing that. We felt awful
and didn't know what to do but the other day
a lady from our Church drove out to call
and a little bird knocked itself out while she sat
and she brought it in her hands right into the house,
it looked like dead. It had a kind of hat
of feathers sticking up on its head, kind of rose
or pinky color, don't know what it was,
and I petted it and it come to life right there
in her hands and she took it out and it flew. She says
they think the window is the sky on a fair
day, she feeds birds too but hasn't got
so many. She says to hang strips of aluminum foil

in the window so we'll do that. She raved about
our birds. P.S. The book just come in the mail.

v

Say, that book is sure good, I study
in it every day and enjoy our birds.
Some of them I can't identify
for sure, I guess they're females, the Latin words
I just skip over. Bet you'd never guess
the sparrows I've got here, House Sparrows you wrote,
but I have Fox Sparrows, Song Sparrows, Vesper Sparrows,
Pine Woods and Tree and Chipping and White Throat
and White Crowned Sparrows. I have six Cardinals,
three pairs, they come at early morning and night,
the males at the feeder and on the ground the females.
Juncos, maybe 25, they fight
for the ground, that's what they used to call snowbirds. I miss
the Bluebirds since the weather warmed. Their breast
is the color of a good ripe muskmelon. Tufted Titmouse
is sort of blue with a little tiny crest.
And I have Flicker and Red-Bellied and Red-
Headed Woodpeckers, you would die laughing
to see Red-Bellied, he hangs on with his head
flat on the board, his tail braced up under,
wing out. And Dickcissel and Ruby Crowned Ringlet
and Nuthatch stands on his head and Veery on top
the color of a bird dog and Hermit Thrush with spot
on breast, Blue Jay so funny, he will hop
right on the backs of the other birds to get the grain.
We bought some sunflower seeds just for him.
And Purple Finch I bet you never seen,
color of a watermelon, sits on the rim
of the feeder with his streaky wife, and the squirrels,
you know, they are cute too, they sit tall
and eat with their little hands, they eat bucketfuls.
I pulled my own tooth, it didn't bleed at all.

VI

It's sure a surprise how well Mother is doing,
she forgets her laxative but bowels move fine.
Now that windows are open she says our birds sing
all day. The girl took a Book of Knowledge on loan
from the library and I am reading up
on the habits of birds, did you know some males have three
wives, some migrate some don't. I am going to keep
feeding all spring, maybe summer, you can see
they expect it. Will need thistle seed for Goldfinch and Pine
Siskin next winter. Some folks are going to come see us
from Church, some bird watchers, pretty soon.
They have birds in town but nothing to equal this.

So the world woos its children back for an evening kiss.

I was fortunate enough to have
a mother who on one occasion
encouraged me by commissioning
a poem. Newly married, I
was tackling my first teaching job
when a letter came which said, in part:
"As writing is so easy for you
I want you to write a poem about
the San Benito Ladies Auxiliary
that I belong to. Our club has twenty
members and we bake cute cookies
and serve them with coffee and do our sewing
at the meeting. We make stuffed animals
to give poor Texas kids at Xmas.
We meet on every other Wednesday.
Tell all that in the poem. Write
the poem to be sung to the tune
of Silent Night Holy Night
as that is the only song I have learned
to play so far on my accordion.
I want to play and sing it at
the club meeting. I could do it myself
of course but writing makes me nervous.
I'm sure you will do this for me because
it is so easy for you and I know
you wouldn't want me to get nervous.
I have to have it this week so I
can get it down pat for the next meeting."

In the midst of grading a hundred or so
freshman themes, trying to master
A Vision so I could teach Yeats, and reading
the output of my creative writing
class, I wrote the poem for her.
(Some of the rhymes were hard.) I'm only
sorry that I didn't keep
a copy, and that I missed the performance.

7

SPEAK, MEMORY!*

For once she gets to go with big Cousin Beatie,
who is starting her breasts. They're at Uncle Charlie's farm.
Grandma says, "Ach, Kind, what will they think of next
enahow, the town school? Hunt the butterflies, yet!"
But Beatie says, "It's an *Assignment*."

Mother says, "Now *go*, first." But she hates the outhouse,
where you have to close yourself in with the awful stink
or the collie will try to lick you while you sit on the hole.
Aunt Cora has made two nets from wire and cheesecloth,
and they each take a net and a canning jar.

"How many kinds of butterflies are there, Beatie?"
"I don't know. I have to make a *Collection*."
They're on flowers. "Where are some flowers, Beatie?"
(Mother has beds of bachelor buttons and cosmos.)
"Along there." "Where?" "Right *there*, dumbbell."

Between the road and the cornfield (now she can see)
humps of dust and sand turn to black-eyed Susans,
thistle, goldenrod, clover. And a little white flutter.
"There's one! Run!" Down and out of the ditch,
thrashing through scratchy weeds. Run!

It zigs to the cornfield, lifts overhead. "Oh, shoot!"
They walk and walk. The sun burns down. The cornfields
rustle beside them. A car goes bumping by,
throwing clouds of stinging dust over their sweat.
There. A white one. Run! "I *got* him!"

The sun burns. "These are all the same,
let's look in the pasture." They hold the bob-wire for each
other.

* *This poem refers to, and partly depends upon, for its similarities and
its ironic contrasts, another version of a writer's childhood—Vladimir
Nabokov's in* Speak, Memory!

Gnats fly up and stick on her wet skin.
"There's some more white ones." Run! She trips over burdock,
slips on cow-pies. *"I got one!"*

(Where are the black-striped big ones she's seen at home?)
It's hard to breathe. The sun pounds on her head.
Itch-bumps and dirt mottle her arms and legs.
Devil's pitchforks pock her anklets. Hummocks trip her.
Grasshoppers rattle up in her face.

The red-and-white cows munch and mourn, but won't hurt you.
Sweat runs under wet bangs and into eyes.
They sit in the shade of a tree for a while. "My butterflies
got sort of broken." "There's some more white ones." Run!
(Mother won't like the rip in her bloomers.)

"We better go home." "How many we got?" "Seven,
but they're all the same." "Well, one of 'em's almost yellow."
"Heck, there ain't any other kind around here. I'll flunk
my *Assignment.*" "Gee!" Her feet fall into road ruts,
she burns and chills all the way back.

Through the back yard where the hens huddle in dust holes,
around the slimy white mud where dishwater's thrown,
through swarms of flies at the door, and into the house
with its flies, its faint, strawy smell of cow manure,
its kerosene lamps and Congoleum flowers.

The parrot is calling the dogs in Aunt Cora's voice,
"Here Rover, here Sport!" and whistling them "wheet, wheet,
    wheet,"
(Mother calls her cockers Togo and Peewee)
and the silly farm dogs are coming on a panting run.
It's nearly time for bread-and-milk supper.

Grandma says, "Gott in Himmel, look the poor Kinder!"
They pump pee-colored rainwater to cool their faces
at the tin-lined sink. Cleopatra, Oak Eggars, Tortoiseshell,
Speckled Woods, Eupthecia nabokovi,
where were you that hot day in Iowa?

They had the Boston Bull before I was born,
and Mother liked her far more than she liked me.
We both had a trick. When Mother shaved one forefinger
with the other and said, "Shame, *sha-a-me!*" Peewee
would growl and snap most amusingly right on cue.
I, when shamed in the same manner, would cry.
I see my error now, but what good does it do?

PHOTOGRAPHS

"Take what you want, we'll throw the rest away.
The mice are building nests in the box, we don't
want that old stuff anymore." My father, 88,
kicks the box over to me with his good leg.
My mother sits on her pee-damp paper pad,
trying to take part. The box is jammed to the top
with photos and albums, dust and chewed-up rug wool.
I dump and sort. Their parents' wedding pictures
scorched on cardboard where dimly and patiently
they held their breaths and posed for the sulphurous flash—
the men perched rigid in wicker studio chairs,
the girls standing beside in long, dark,
serviceable, handsewn gowns, their faces
stiff and startled as a dahlia presented
in a frill of ruching or of tatted lace,
one hand on the husband's shoulder, where it stayed.
Then with their broods of children, young, half-grown,
grown, their faces turning stern, parental,
bodies swelling, then melting down. "Surely
you want this batch." My parents shake their heads.
They are nobody's children now, or mine perhaps.

Their brothers and sisters, the fat, self-righteous face
of Grace, the missionary, who told me, eight
years old, "You're a bad, *bad* girl to say 'my goodness.'
Do you know why?" "No." "Because Goodness is GOD!"
May, the educated one, capped, gowned,
adopted by a rich and childless aunt
and given "advantages." Brought back for dinner
once with her own siblings, she laughed and cried out,
pointing at Dad, "Look at that boy's big nose!"—
a story my father told with bitterness
till he was in his sixties. Cora, whose faith-healer
couldn't cure the cancer she hid from her doctor.
Brownie, whose beautiful dark eyes were closed
to near-blindness by their drooping lids when she fell

downstairs and struck her head as a young bride.
Al, lover of poop-pillows, plastic turds
and pop-up snakes, whose youthful high-jinks
twisted to drunkenness and kleptomania.
The others, too, outlived. "I'll take all these."
Their web of love and hate has been broomed away.

"Who's this young woman?" My mother holds the picture
up to her eyes and squints her best. Dad takes it.
"Oh, *I* know, Anna Meinberg, Mother's chum.
When I was courting I always had to bring
a man for Anna or Mother wouldn't go."
He laughs toward Mother, but she doesn't smile.
"Throw it away." They are not lovers now.

I sort in the dimming light. My mother dozes.
'Who are all these children, Dad?" "Must be
your mother's folks, some Richsmeier or Peters kids."
They sit patiently, brushed, told to hold still,
their legs in black stockings and feet in high-top shoes
stuck out in front of them, the button-eyed
babies in crocheted caps with ribbon pom-poms
on either ear, sacked in tucked gowns or naked
like rubber dolls, their faces plump possibility.
For all three of us, they go in a discard pile.

And now a precious stack, my parents themselves:
The boy with his plowing team, the young father
with pompadour, the deep family lines
already scored between brows. ("When I grow up
I'm going to marry Daddy!" Then Mother's jealous
"Well you can't. *I* married him." "Why can't
I marry him too?" "Because you *can't*, that's why!")
Posed proudly with his bantams, with his turkeys,
goats (he never lost his farmer's heart).
Small eyes that never saw another's pain
or point of view ("Your mother's always complaining.

I've fed and clothed her all her life. What more
does she *want?*") Full lips that laid down the law for us.
Big feeder before his heart attack, his Santa
belly swells in the gas station uniform.
"You'll have to feed him good," his mother told
his bride. "If dinner's late just hurry and set
the table. He'll think the food is almost ready."
Pride in the stances. "My word's my bond. I've never
cheated man nor woman." Pride of place:
"All that education will make you Big-Headed."
"All that reading will make you lose your mind."
My mother, the youngest, the beauty of her clan,
minx who wooed big brother Al away
from Cora, his twin, and held him clutched lifelong
in mischief and complicity. Expressive
face I studied all my childhood to learn
if I was wrong or right, kept or cast out.
Best cook in town, best seamstress—not enough.
"I'd have been a great singer if I hadn't married."
"I could have been a nurse if I hadn't had you."
In a ruffled dustcap, her arms and lap piled full
of eleven puppies, then standing with a braid
of thick hair down to her knees, then bobbed, marcelled,
then permed—the lovely features never show
her "nerves," the long years of dissatisfaction,
the walks she took me on when I reached adolescence
and poured my hard ear full of my father's failings.
"Don't tell *me* about it, it's not my fault,
I didn't marry him!" "Mother, wake up.
I wish you could see this picture of your long hair."
"I could *sit* on my hair." The old boast comes by rote.
"You want to keep this batch a little longer, don't you?"
"No." Those faces have turned fictional.

And now their only child, long-legged, skinny
from trying to please and hardly ever pleasing.
Long curls my mother wound on rags for a while,

then highschool ugliness, then a fragile gauze
of beauty young womanhood laid on the lens, then lifted,
with my young husband slowly changing beside me,
my father's face stamped clearer and clearer on mine,
sterile publicity pictures, graying hair.
I need not ask the two frail watchers my question.
They are no longer parents. Their child is old.

The last's my ace—my father's great adventure.
Suddenly he bought a housetrailer and pulled
his startled family from our Iowa village,
out of the cornfields and into the world's wonders,
all the way to Washington, then down
the California coast, then back to home,
packing a trunk so full of memories
they've lasted him for nearly fifty years.
The earth erupted for us all in moonscapes
of Black Hills, mountaintops hung from the sky
(the old Pontiac boiling on every pass),
Salt Lake held you up without an inner tube,
rodeos bucked in Wyoming, bears rocked the trailer
at night in National Parks, great waterfalls roared,
Mother and I made snowballs in July
on Crater Lake and posed before studios
in Hollywood, we all stood on Boulder Dam,
our fan belt broke in the desert and Dad hitchhiked
while I fainted from the heat. On the desert, too,
in the one hundred twenty degree trailer, Mother
boiled potatoes and made gravy for dinner.
"If I don't get my spuds every noon I'll drive
us right back home!" We knew he meant what he said.
For years we all re-lived the trip, Dad using
the album to remind himself of stories,
used it to entertain any company—
old friends, then new ones elsewhere—then, years later,
the hired help of their old age. Still later
I'd use it to get him going, to cheer him up,

to distract him from worries, boredom, aches and pains.
I turn on the light. "Dad, here's our *trip!* Remember. . . ."
He interrupts, staring at the darkened window,
"Everything's rusting away out in the garage.
It's been so long since I could get outside . . ."
My mother stirs. "When's the girl going to fix
my banana and coffee? I want to go back to bed."
I close the box. Somewhere a telephone
has made the appointment—a flower-scented pose
where they wait with patience for one witnessing heart
to snap its picture of their final faces.

THE STREAM

for my mother

Four days with you, my father three months dead.
You can't tell months from years, but you feel sad,

and you hate the nursing home. I've arranged a lunch
for the two of us, and somehow you manage to pinch

the pin from Madrid I bought you closed at the neck
of your best red blouse, put on new slacks, and take

off your crocheted slippers to put on shiny shoes,
all by yourself. "I don't see how you could close

that pin. You look so nice!" "Well, I tried and tried,
and worked till I got it. They didn't come," you said.

"Mother, I'm sorry, this is the wrong day,
our lunch is tomorrow. Here's a big kiss anyway

for dressing up for me. The nurse will come in
tomorrow and help you put on your clothes and pin."

"These last few days her mind has certainly cleared.
Of course the memory's gone," your doctor said.

Next day they bathed you, fixed your hair and dressed
you up again, got a wheelchair and wheeled you past

the fat happy babbler of nonsense who rolled her chair
all day in the hall, the silent stroller who wore

a farmer's cap and bib overalls with rows
of safety pins on the bib, rooms of old babies

in cribs, past the dining hall, on down to a sunny
lounge in the other wing. "Where can I pee,

if I have to pee? I don't like it here, I'm afraid.
Where's my room? I'm going to faint," you said.

But they came with the lunch and card table and chairs
and bustled and soothed you and you forgot the fears

and began to eat. The white tablecloth, the separate
plate for salad, the silvery little coffee pot,

the covers for dishes must have made you feel
you were in a restaurant again after all

those shut-in years. (Dad would never spend the money,
but long ago you loved to eat out with me.)

You cleaned your soup bowl and dishes, one by one,
and kept saying, "This is fun! This is *fun!*"

The cake fell from your trembly fork, so I fed
it to you. "Do you want mine, too?" "Yes," you said,

"and I'll drink your milk if you don't want it." (You'd
lost twelve pounds already by refusing your food.)

I wheeled you back. "Well, I never did *that* before!
Thank you, Jane." "We'll do it again." "Way down *there*,"

you marveled. You thanked me twice more. My eyes were wet.
"You're welcome, Mother. You'll have a good nap now, I'll
bet."

I arranged for your old companion, who came twice a day,
to bring you milkshakes, and reached the end of my stay.

On the last night I helped you undress. Flat dugs
like antimacassars lay on your chest, your legs

and arms beetle-thin swung from the swollen belly
(the body no more misshapen, no stranger to see,

after all, at the end than at the beloved beginning).
You chose your flowered nightgown as most becoming.

You stood at the dresser, put your teeth away,
washed your face, smoothed on Oil of Olay,

then Avon night cream, then put Vicks in your nose,
then lay on the bed. I sat beside your knees

to say goodbye for a month. "You know I'll call
every Sunday and write a lot. Try to eat well—"

Tears stopped my voice. With a girl's grace you sat up
and, as if you'd done it lifelong, reached out to cup

my face in both your hands, and, as easily
as if you'd said it lifelong, you said, "Don't cry,

don't cry. You'll never know how much I love you."
I kissed you and left, crying. It felt true.

I forgot to tell them that you always sneaked your meat,
you'd bragged, to the man who ate beside you. One night

at home, my heart ringing with what you'd said,
then morning, when the phone rang to say you were dead.

I see your loving look wherever I go.
What is love? Truly I do not know.

Sometimes, perhaps, instead of a great sea,
it is a narrow stream running urgently

far below ground, held down by rocky layers,
the deeds of mother and father, helpless sooth-sayers

of how our life is to be, weighted by clay,
the dense pressure of thwarted needs, the replay

of old misreadings, by hundreds of feet of soil,
the gifts and wounds of the genes, the short or tall

shape of our possibilities, seeking
and seeking a way to the top, while above, running

and stumbling this way and that on the clueless ground,
another seeker clutches a dowsing-wand

which bends, then lifts, dips, then straightens, everywhere,
saying to the dowser, it is there, it is not there,

and the untaught dowser believes, does not believe,
and finally simply stands on the ground above,

till a sliver of stream finds a crack and makes its way,
slowly, too slowly, through rock and earth and clay.

Here at my feet I see, after sixty years,
the welling water—to which I add these tears.

THE CASE OF THE

Drinking the seconal dissolved in bourbon,
stabbed in the fog, shoved into quicksand,
caught in the telescopic sight,
feeling a sudden pressure on the carotids from behind,

scalped, buried, bombed, smothered in cellophane,
"another blow and another, savage, fast,
unreasoning," in Amsterdam,
Gary, Indonesia, Alabama, Budapest,

perilous, perilous the keeping of the human spirit.
Killed everywhere, on the train, in the tomb,
generosity, at the racetrack, grace,
at the tiller, down the sewers, in the unguarded hospital room,

willingness, in the London slum, on the plane,
at the mountain resort, strength, in the pew,
on Golden Gate Bridge, affection. Nowhere to hide.
Everywhere, everywhere someone is out looking for you.

One, with his mouth hung open to hear,
grunts "Huh?" after every statement. "*Huh?*"
His prostate swells, blood pressure bangs his head.
"This country's gone to the dogs and the hippies can go too."

And one pees fourteen times a night,
missing the bedpan every other time.
Her false teeth clicking with malice, she whispers,
"If you don't watch them every minute they'll *steal you blind.*"

Are the passersby in collusion? Did the victim
deserve what he got? The search for evidence
goes on and on, the light burns,
the sirens whine, the long report says you only live once.

Fingerprints, autopsies, exhumations
tell us a great deal, but the shoes
don't fit anyone we know. As for the bodies,
some were fair of face, some had nothing to lose.

On the last page, the one-eyed witness,
trapped by the D.A., drops his dreams and his lies,
his squirrel mouth opens, and he squeals all he knows:
"The sun done it, coming up every damn morning like it does!"

warted, once upon a time,
waiting a kiss to tell him he too
could be beloved. My frog,
my frog, where shall I find you?

I learned of its very real enhancement.
That was a little harder. I had a ball
before I learned to use what beauty I had
with kindness and honor. That was hardest of all.
Our son was born, and I went to the child
through a clutter of nursemaids to tell him
how it feels to be poor. I started to grow old.
My husband saw everything and was grateful.
Thickening a bit at the waist, he firmed
and stayed, always, faithful.

And that was the second transformation,
slow and solid.
We were happy together.

Everything comes in three's, they say,
and I'm stuck in the third transformation,
flopping like a fish who's out of the life-saving
everyday water. I starve now for a ration
of dreams, I've never learned to live
without dreams. All through the filth and anger
of childhood I ate them like a calming sugar,
my sweet secret. I move through the palace,
gripping its ghostly furniture
till my fingers ache. I guess
that it is real, that I am living,
but what is there left to dream of?
I dream, day and night, of giving.

Prince, soon to be king,
we've made all our lovely exchanges
and my years as your princess are ending.
Couldn't there be, for me,
just one more fairytale?
More fiercely than the silliest clubwoman
in the kingdom, I try to hold onto my looks
because I dream that there was someone

THERE

IN THE MISSOURI OZARKS

Under an overwashed, stiff, gray
sheet of sky, the hills
lie like a litter of woodchucks,
their backs mottled black with leafless
branches and brown with oakleaves,
hanging on till spring.
Little towns are scabs in their haunches.

Out of the hills the pickups scuttle
like water beetles onto the highway,
which offers up STUCKEY'S, EATS,
GOD'S WELL, CAVES,
JUNQUE, HOT BISCUITS 'N'
CREAM GRAVY, $6. OVERNIGHT
CABINS and a WINERY
to the chilled traveller.

Town leads off with a garish motel,
followed by the Shopping Plaza—
a monster of a supermarket
and a few frail shops; then comes
the courthouse square, with a barnfaced
Dollar Department Store,
Happy's Hardware and TV,
Shorty's Beer-Cafe,
two quiet banks and a chiropractor.
Big white gingerbreaded houses
and new ranchstyles
fizzle out on the edge of town
to yellow, brickpatterned tarpaper
shacks, leaning against the firewood
stacked as high as their roofs.

Off the highway, frosty weeds
lift berries and pods
on either side of the road in a mileslong

wine and black and beige bouquet,
and every twenty acres or so
a fieldstone cottage
guards its pastured cows
and its woods of oak and black walnut.
Farm dogs explode from porches
and harry the car down the gravel,
yipping at stones spat from the wheels.
Out here, after the supper dishes,
three or four couples will walk down the road
to a neighbor's, and will sit
around the heating stove,
talking about Emma Harbis,
who is finally giving away cuttings
of her famous orange-blooming
Kalanchoë, and about the Ed Lelands,
on food stamps all year,
but with a brand new pickup
parked bold as brass
in their front yard, and about
Old Lady Kerner, who was seen
in the drugstore buying Oil of Olay
to smooth out the wrinkles
eighty-two hard years have hammered
into her indomitable face.

MOOSE IN THE MORNING, NORTHERN MAINE

At six A.M. the log cabins
nose an immense cow-pie of mist
that lies on the lake.
Nineteen pale goldfinches perch
side by side on the telephone wire
that runs to shore,
and under them the camp cow,
her bones pointing this way and that,
is collapsed like a badly-constructed
pup tent in the dark weeds.
Inside, I am building a fire
in the old woodstove with its rod overhead
for hunters' clothes to steam on.
I am hunting for nothing—
perhaps the three cold pencils
that lie on the table like kindling
could go in to start the logs.
I remember Ted Weiss saying,
"At the exhibition I suddenly realized
Picasso had to re-make everything he laid his eyes on
into an art object.
He couldn't let the world alone.
Since then I don't write every morning."

The world is warming and lightening
and mist on the pond
dissolves into bundles and ribbons.
At the end of my dock there comes clear,
bared by the gentle burning,
a monstrous hulk with thorny head,
up to his chest in the water,
mist wreathing round him.
Grander and grander grows the sun
until he gleams, his brown coat
glistens, the great rack,
five feet wide, throws sparks

of light. A ton of monarch,
munching, he stands spotlit.
Then slowly, gravely, the great neck lowers
head and forty pounds of horn
to sip the lake.
The sun stains the belittled
cow's hide amber.
She heaves her bones and bag
and her neckbell gongs
as she gets to her feet
in yellow blooms of squaw-weed.
On the telephone wire
all the little golden bells are ringing
as that compulsive old scribbler, the universe,
jots down another day.

THE HERMIT OF HUDSON POND

"Like most of the hermits in the area
[he] obeyed to the letter the Fish and Game Laws."

In the "immaculately neat" cabin it is calm and warm.
Deermice with Disney ears run the rafters by day
and rustle, gnaw and squeak in the provisions at night.
The snowshoe rabbit, red in sun as a setter,
hops and sits, twitching its nose, outside the door,
and all around, from trees to ground, the air
flashes with the yellow and black and white flight
of Evening Grosbeaks, fat with the spruce budworms
they feed on. The pond, like a great pan of broth,
bubbles with feeding trout when the hatch comes on.
For forty years, the days dawn and darken
in quiet order for the hermit of Hudson Pond,
only one law reaching in to his natural place.
No women with their feverish voices and strange, bloody days,
nor men, murdering, hustling, re-making the world,
only the self trimmed to its simplest needs,
shelter, food, for friendship a dog, and the days
dawning and darkening on woods and pond,
the moose wading in, mergansers churning the water
like motorboats as they scoot for a fish, loon
hooting and yodeling, or, when the snow comes,
the deep, still white, the burning, glistering cold.

"June 9, 1961" the flying service pilot
checks on the hermit and finds a note in the cabin:

"I killed myself because I had to kill
my baby dog for chasing deer. I threw
my pistol into the lake after I shot
baby dog. I didn't have nerve enough
to shoot myself. I didn't have to shoot
my dog. No one knew she was chasing deer
but me. I want to suffer because I think

29

it was a crime to shoot my baby dog.
If you find this, Ray, I'm all done living. I'm on
the bottom of the lake beside my dog."

Quotes from Anne Howe, "Hermits of the Moosehead Region,"
MOOSEHEAD, MAINE BICENTENNIAL BOOKLET, 1976

MADRID, 1974

I

All the world is walking on the Gran Via,
we too, locked into step in the evening parade:
double-breasted businessmen in blocky trios,
slinky sweethearts, grandmas in black with faces like wintered-
over apples, longhairs humped by backpacks,
couples with the kids, the babybuggies and the perros.
Buildings along both sides are layer cakes
of light—from all levels alert leather shops,
doll shops, paella parlors, one-floor
hotels and beauty salons dangle with hope
their tiny, hard-to-find elevators.
The crowd compresses where cafe tables fly outdoors
and settle on the Avenida and where lines are forming
under marquees that translate "Deliverance" or "The Sting."
A stream of vowels that all the world shouts
flows over the pebblebacks of cars rolling down the center.
And yet, already, more than a block away
from our own cafe, where she locates herself, I can hear her,
AW-EE-AW (surely she has swallowed a foghorn), her bray,
above the honk and hubbub, the voice of a giantess
invoking chance in a strange language, the voice of my Muse.

II

At our home cafe we're sipping Schweppes limon.
Regulars here are having their pastry and coffee
(as regulars in bars in the Old Town
are having grilled shrimp, sausage, squid and wine,
and children in plazas are running with a sugar bun
in one hand, and teens at corner counters are gulping
their "hot little dogs.") It is eight o'clock. Dinner's at eleven.
Our local gigolo, with purse and cane,
sits with a hennaed matron, then with a bleached one.
Guitar-slung, our hippie hustles pesetas for a hostel.
Against the glass front our elegant shoe-shine
gentleman leans at ease. Our favorite sign

31

Madrid, 1974

across the street lights up: EL EDEN DE LOS
  PANTALONES.
But it is she, our lottery lady, who gives life and tone
to the place. On other corners cripples and crones
whine and sell the touch of a wen or a humped back,
but she's square and light on her feet as a box of Corn Kix.
Wide bosom flapping with tickets, embodied luck,
she flirts at each table. They feed her forkfuls of cake.
She sweats, slaps at flies and smiles. She'll shoot out like a bee
at the passers, light on someone, and exchange a joke.
All the world laughs with her. When a table is empty
she'll scrub it dry with her hand out of sheer energy.
The waiters wink. Often she'll stand and yell,
voice aimed at the whole city, at farmer, at gypsy
in the mountains beyond: EE-AW, come to me and all will be
  well.

III

Four flights overhead they're cooking our half-pension meal.
How I love the cold crunch of Gazpacho, the wry red wine,
the shiny green and black olives and their oil,
the Huevos Flamenca, the tick of a fork on a seashell
in the saffron rice, the Sangria aswirl with sliced lemon
and apple, the sugary oranges, the musky sting
of the brandy! How I love, like a Spanish king,
El Greco, Goya, El Bosco, Zurburan,
the stagey Plaza Mayor, the swarming Puerta del Sol—
in fact, except for the corrida, everything, everything!
In the loteria of grants my number came up.
Skimming olivegroves spattered with poppies, the plane did not
  fall.
For more than a thousand days I have not been ill.
Some dear ones are still alive. The world is full,
and its servant, the word, through art's little ee-aw-ee,
praises its fullness in every lucky country.

MADRID, MAY, 1977

"Spain will surprise you." SUAREZ

Tooting down the Gran Via,
tossing out bundles of loose white leaflets,
the campaign caravans roll.
At nine in the evening
leaflets snow on the heads and shoulders
of Madrilenos at sidewalk cafes
and cover their plates of hot, fried churros,
while those in the paseo scuff through leaflets stained with
streetdust and churro grease.
Mornings, out of each porteria pops
a porter with broom like a jack-in-the-box
to bare his section of the street
for a few hours until the tooting begins
again, and the paper snow.
It is a serious carnival.

The waiter who speaks English
and looks like a sad prizefighter
sets down my plate of langostinos
and says, "Yes, we have learned
very quickly how to disagree.
The hardest thing we must learn now
is how to disagree without violence."

Off the main streets we walk in a city
of paper walls, one hundred
and fifty-nine parties have built these surfaces
of pasted paper and print.
Like bears on hind legs sharpening their claws,
men and women stand by the walls
and scratch with their fingernails
at the campaign posters they disagree with,
ripping tiny strips from the print.
We pass a five-year-old,
scraping with his nails at a poster.

This is a new game.
Only people over sixty-two have
ever played it before.

In the evening stroll, young lovers in jeans,
twined together like churros,
writhe through double-breasted businessmen,
past posters of La Pasionaria,
past bare breasts blooming on news kiosks,
past movie lines for uncensored sex.
For good or ill, America strolls up the street.

At midnight, coming from supper,
we stop at a gray clump on the sidewalk.
It is a pile of puppies.
They are asleep,
cuddled together on the pavement
in a litter of leaflets.
Off to one side, their owner
dickers with three possible customers,
each of whom has for a moment forgotten
that, in a few weeks, having placed
a slip of paper in a plastic urn,
into his empty right hand will fall
responsibility for his own life
and a share of responsibility for the world.

It was gray.
There was no gruel
for hours, years.
All around me
drone of a
dead world.
Dry cold rocks
in my bed,
rocks of hours, years.
The skin sank
to the skeleton
and stuck,
dry.

Then
the steam of celery
soaked my face clean.
A lump of potato
lit
on the back of my tongue,
warm weight.
The stock
seeped into sockets
and soothed
my bones.
The onion
clawed open
my nose.
My eyes
consumed the bowl
whole.
The red beans
rolled under my gums
and the carrots were blazing
with life, with *life*.

AT PÈRE LACHAISE

What began as death's avenue
becomes, as we go on,
death's village, then metropolis,
and the four of us,
reading our rain-blistered Michelin
map of graves, keep looking back,
but cafés, tabacs,
boulangeries are gone.
It is a long way yet
to where we are going to please me,
and the bunch of muguets
I am holding too tightly is frayed
already. On either side
of the cobbles we slip on,
darkly arched over by dripping chestnuts,
the ten foot high deathhouses
stand, and we can see
at hilltop intersections
only further suburbs of
the imposing dead.
For a while we are lost
in this silent city—
the map is not detailed
and the avenues curve.
It is cold here. I am very cold.
My friend begins to cry.
We find a Kleenex for her
and a tranquilizer.
Head bent, hand clenched
to her mouth, her black bob
spattered with chestnut petals,
she stumbles and turns her ankle.
I am to blame.
A whole afternoon in Paris spent
on this spooky pilgrimage,
and we are too far in to go back.

The rain has stopped.
"Look, my God, *look!*"
Anything awful can happen here,
but I look where she points.
Ahead, at a break in the trees
where a weak ray of sun shines through,
two of the great dun tombs
are dappled with color, with cats,
more cats than I can believe,
two dozen at least,
sitting or lying on doorsills,
window ledges, pedestals, roofs,
and a yellow one, high in the air,
curled round at rest on the bar
of a towering cross.
Grimalkins, grandpas,
lithe rakes, plump dowagers,
princes, peasants, old warriors, hoydens,
gray, white, black, cream, orange,
spotted, striped and plain—
a complete society of cats,
posed while we stand and stare.
My heart is thumping.
"Are we dreaming?
Oh, aren't they beautiful!"
my friend whispers.
We smile at the cats for a long time
before we go on past.
We are almost there.

Off to the side,
behind the grand monuments,
we find a flat slab marked MARCEL PROUST
and, feeling a little foolish,
I lay my fistsized white bouquet
on his black marble.

We go back another way
where the street widens,
opening out to gardens,
and we run down broad steps,
laughing at nothing.
A few people appear,
arranging gladioli in urns,
and far down the hill we can see
an exit to the boulevard.
We find Colette's grave
on the way out and call to her,
"You should have seen the cats!"

HERE

THE LEARNERS

We slapped the smirking mother
and the swollen father
and went to live in museums
and anthologies. Around us
were images of such fairness
that the world outside
was smoothed into smog.
We knew it was hard.
We were bony and strong
but our knuckles broke
as we cleaned and copied.

When rocks split the cellophane windows
we stumbled outside
leading the eldest.
Sun seared our eyeballs
and the cramp of the journey
crazed some of the seemliest.
Some of us dried to jerky.
When the light lowered a bit
some of us said they found
beauty beyond belief
in the ashes and oilspills.

When darkness came down
some mated, some murdered each other.
Some of us shook our fists
at the moon and the stars
for disdainful distance.
All over creation
there were sounds and shadows.
Digging into a cockpit of earth
with our broken knuckles
some of us sat and waited
with whatever was in the world.

RINGLING BROTHERS, BARNUM AND BAILEY

Thirty striped rumps in a circle with tails dangling.
One rump lifts and begins to dump, then spray.
At the crack of the cue, still pissing, she leaps to the ring
with the others and they all stand on their hind legs pawing
the air for balance. The dwarf on ten foot stilts
keeps stalking around the show, his little hands
waving, and we all wave every time round, and he tilts
to one side and staggers but now everybody is watching
the pony walk on his hind legs round and round
the kneeling camels while the whip flicks his strained belly.
Then, hanging by one wrist only, the aerialist spins
her whole body over . . . fifty times. "That's easy,
I could do that," the child behind me whines.
Directly overhead the tight rope walkers
work in a hush. (Three days from now one will smash
to her death in another town.) Absent watchers
are my two friends, one in the last months
of cancer, one in depression so deep she'll crash.
One leaps over the other. The rope holds. No one killed
today. "Anybody could do that. So what?"
the child whines, and I'd like to throw the child
and all brutal innocence under the elephant's foot.

CARING FOR SURFACES

Birds build but not I build, no, but wipe, Time's wife.
Dipped in detergent, dish and chandelier retrieve
their glister, sopped, kitchen floor reflowers, knife
rubbed with cork unrusts, colors of carpetweave
cuffed with shampooer and vacuum will reblush,
prints sprayed and scrubbed no longer peer but stare,
buffed, silver burns, brushed, plaster will gush
hue at you, tops soothed with cloth will clear.

Cleansing the cloud from windows, I let the world win.
It comes in, and its light and heat heave the house,
discolor, dim, darken my surfaces. Then once again,
as for forty years, my fingers must make them rouse.

Round rooms of surfaces I move, round board, books, bed.
Men carve, dig, break, plunge as I smooth, shine, spread.

To tell you the truth, the shoe pinched.
I had no way of knowing, you see,
that I was the girl he'd dreamed of.
Imagination had always consoled me,
but I'd tried to use it with care.
My sisters, I'd always thought, were the family
romantics, expecting nice clothes to do the trick
instead of the beholder's transforming eye.
All that dancing I would have to have done,
if it *was* me, had made my feet swollen.
But I didn't know I'd been dancing, I thought him a dreamer.
He had everything—looks, loneliness,
the belief that comforting and love could cure
even an advanced neurosis.
I didn't know whether or not
he was deluded, but I was sure
he was brave. I wanted to have worn the slipper.

And that's all there was to the first transformation,
something that happened so fast I nearly lost it
with one disclaiming murmur, but something
that did happen, that he made me believe.

None of my skills but love was the slightest use
to my husband. Others did well at keeping
the home fires damped or hot.
And so I began to learn the sleeping
senses. I learned wholly to love
the man in the prince, what didn't dance:
bad breath in the morning, sexual clumsiness,
a childlike willingness to let the old queen
dominate. That was easy. And I read a lot.
Snarled in ideas, heading for the unseen,
I heard the wise men snicker when I spoke.
I learned that I had some beauty and, wearing
one gown or another for my husband's sake,

SALESWOMEN IN BAKERY SHOPS

touch gently
with the tips of their
floured white fingers.

Round-faced and neat,
spry hair netted down,
they feel frosted with chocolate.

They move in a brightness
of raspberry,
in a warm flurry of
crust-flakes and ground almonds.

They smile with their apricot lips
and speak in a vanilla voice.
Radiance of ovens reflects on their cheeks.

They rest their eyes on
yeasty beds,
pillows of beaten eggwhite.
Lemon tingles
between their breasts.

Carefully, carefully they proffer
sugared shapes,
fragile twists,
soft sponge cups.

No sour returns
to scrape them,
no rape of goods.

Everything wild
is sweetened out of them.

Their tender transactions are finished
before the buttery dough
blotches the white sack
on the way home.

FALL

For James, who liked it

Here's that old drunk, already mellow.
A few nips and he's at his best.
Everything brightens up. Summer,
who can't stand him, gets somebody to take her
home. (She's spoiled and tired.) The rest
cluster around and enjoy his show.
Actually, they're the same jokes,
the one about the travelling mercury
and the farmer's pumpkins, the same tricks,
lighting bittersweet and sumac
without a match. Well, those who can't be
original can be good old boys.
A wall mural in lipstick, and he's back
at the bar. Now for those boozy tears,
you know they come from a cold will.
And now, for God's sake, one of his rages.
He's storming around, knocking down everything,
leaves, lovers, lights, stepping
on chrysanthemums. It seems ages
since he's been this bad. Then his brow clears
and he gives us his look: "Aren't I a smarty?"
Soon he'll pass out. Appalling! Still,
he's always welcome at the next party.

THE VISION TEST

My driver's license is lapsing and so I appear
in a roomful of waiting others and get in line.
I must master a lighted box of far or near,
a highway language of shape, squiggle and sign.
As the quarter-hours pass I watch the lady in charge
of the test, and think how patient, how slow, how nice
she is, a kindly priestess indeed, her large,
round face, her vanilla pudding, baked-apple-and-spice
face in continual smiles as she calls each "Dear"
and "Honey" and shows first-timers what to see.
She enjoys her job, how pleasant to be in her care
rather than brute little bureaucrat or saleslady.
I imagine her life as a tender placing of hands
on her children's hands as they come to grips with the rocks
and scissors of the world. The girl before me stands
in a glow of good feeling. I take my place at the box.
"And how are *you* this lovely morning, Dear?
A few little questions first. Your name?—Your age?—
Your profession?" "Poet." "What?" She didn't hear.
"Poet," I say loudly. The blank pink page
of her face is lifted to me. "*What?*" she says.
"POET," I yell, "P-O-E-T."
A moment's silence. "*Poet?*" she asks. "Yes."
Her pencil's still. She turns away from me
to the waiting crowd, tips back her head like a hen
drinking clotted milk, and her "Ha ha hee hee hee"
of hysterical laughter rings through the room. Again
"Oh, ha ha ha ha ha hee hee."
People stop chatting. A few titter. It's clear
I've told some marvelous joke they didn't quite catch.
She resettles her glasses, pulls herself together,
pats her waves. The others listen and watch.
"And what are we going to call the color of your hair?"
she asks me warily. Perhaps it's turned white
on the instant, or green is the color poets declare,
or perhaps I've merely made her distrust her sight.

"Up to now it's always been brown." Her pencil trembles,
then with an almost comically obvious show
of reluctance she lets me look in her box of symbols
for normal people who know where they want to go.

A WINTER'S TALE, BY A WIFE

Snorting hippopotamus at the lake's bottom, all snoot,
he lies against me, one arm clamping me down to the fate
he fell to after flying high all year unlit,
and over us, on eyelids, in ears, up noses, the steamer makes hot
waves of viral stew, the bed is marshy with flu-sweat.
Doomed, I thought, by his sneeze in my hair, no hypocrite,
nor amphibian either, I stayed snuggled night after night,
renouncing the cool beach of the guestroom bed, but felt hate.

Fiercer than usual, his passion, by a fake of fever, comes,
and his breath, through clogged airholes, must faster bubble and
    foam;
from head to toe my body, temperate, must take the
    unwholesome
smear of his leaking skin, while his huge achey limbs
jerk and lock toward ease, his sore-throat-bugs like gum
clump in my mouth. There's more to marriage than Freud
    could dream.
This dangerous stranger makes it new. My martyrdom
is romance. And he loves me that I do pity him?

Oh no—this hero fears his tragic isolation.
"Come wheeze with me," he thinks, "and like a pair of loons
we'll dive together to the undercover where all is one,
a murk of sameness. Separate, one sick, one well, we again
have to think of each other. A single handkerchief thickens
the plot, so let Kleenex be plucked by both and, clotful, be
    thrown
on both sides of the bed." But if I ail, my black lover's gone.
In a likeness of misery marital platters don't get licked clean.

And how, against his stuffed and swollen swoon, I feel
my lightness, neatness, sleekness of self, how cleanly, how cool
my voice issues from open sinuses! Let me stay well!
If his chest wheeze and purr, his m's turn to b's, my careful
enunciation, my resonance, will comfort, will fill

the fogged air with affectionate sympathy. Let me peel
for a good many more nights the gross from the ethereal,
lie thus lightly, less Caliban than before, more Ariel.

Besides, I get sicker than he does, cough longer, burn hotter,
    hurt more.
In the daytime I wield mops, pump legs, strain toward vigor,
make the dishwasher sterilize us apart, don't open my pores
before I go out, am lavish with Vitamin C (pure
nonsense). Oh the sweet breath that doesn't whistle in my clear
lungs! (It is by loving me that I know me, rather
than by knowing me that I love.) I bring him pills with sincere
concern, feed him and kiss him, but danger, danger is there.

Graying out of the sex culture, too bored to care who
can or can't have twenty-five bangs with a vibrator, you,
ma semblable, can thrill to think of lifting your husband's tissue
with spaghetti tongs. Proust, I thought, was a fantasist, since we
    do
not really invest each detail of our lives with such meaning,
    but now
he's justified, realist supreme—each snuffle I count to know
how close and closer I am to safety. I'll not get the flu,
I'll not—Ucchk—a tickle in my wrinkling throat? *Atchoo!*

In the old brownstone on W. 35th
death is the business,
"the contemplation of decomposing flesh
and smashed bone."
After a breakfast of brioches
with grilled ham and grape thyme jelly,
"the first shot, from behind, got his
shoulder and turned him around.
The second shot, from in front, got him
in the throat and broke his neck."
Lunch is seekh kebab, finished
with raspberries stirred in a
double-boiler mixture of cream, sugar,
egg yolks, sherry and almond extract,
then briefings of Saul, Fred and Orrie
for the tailings, the break-ins,
followed by anchovy fritters,
partridge in casserole
with no olives in the sauce, cucumber
mousse, and Creole curds and cream.
Stoked with Puerto Rican molasses
on buckwheat cakes, or eggs *au*
beurre noir, or corn fritters coated
with wild thyme honey from Greece,
or deviled grilled lamb kidneys,
Archie, the man of action,
goes out to view the corpse.
"The car knocked her flying for ten feet,
then, when she landed, speeded up
and rolled two of its wheels
over her body." He goes out
to get the facts,
returning to curried beef roll,
celery and cantaloupe salad
and blueberry grunt.
Eyes closed, pushing

his lips in and out, Nero Wolfe,
the man of intellect, thinks.
Verbatim reports. He said. She said.
"She was lying naked on the bed,
a silk scarf knotted around her neck.
Her face was no longer pretty."
Then mussel bisque, duck Mondor,
carottes Flamande and chestnut whip.
For Wolfe, from clams to cheese
is an hour and a half.
Interviews. Traps. Schemes. Fingerprints.
Parry and thrust with Inspector Cramer.
At 7 P.M. he goes to the diningroom
for sweetbreads *amandine* in patty shells,
cold green-corn pudding and rhubarb tart.
"At 11:07 P.M.
he was dead on the floor
with a statue on top of him."
Death is the business
in the old brownstone on W. 35th.

But in the kitchen, doing something with
artichokes, or, in his den
in the basement, dreaming over
294 cookbooks on eleven shelves,
Fritz, the real hero, holds up the house,
speaks, three times a day, for life.
"There will be shad roe, *en casserole*,
with anchovy butter. The sheets
of larding will be rubbed with five herbs.
With the cream to cover will be
an onion and three other herbs,
to be removed before serving."

FIRST

THE BALLAD OF BLOSSOM

The lake is known as West Branch Pond.
It is round as a soapstone griddle.
Ten log cabins nose its sand,
with a dining lodge in the middle.

Across the water Whitecap Mountain
darkens the summer sky,
and loons yodel and moose wade in,
and trout take the feathered fly.

At camp two friendly characters
live out their peaceful days
in the flowery clearing edged by firs
and a-buzz with bumble bees:

Alcott the dog, a charming fool
who sniffs out frog and snake
and in clumsy capering will fall
from docks into the lake,

and Blossom the cow, whose yield is vaunted
and who wears the womanly shape
of a yellow carton badly dented
in some shipping mishap,

with bulging sack appended below
where a full five gallons stream
to fill puffshells and make berries glow
in lakes of golden cream.

Her face is calm and purged of thought
when mornings she mows down fern
and buttercup and forget-me-not
and panties on the line.

Afternoons she lies in the shade
and chews over circumstance.
On Alcott nestled against her side
she bends a benevolent glance.

Vacationers climb Whitecap's side,
pick berries, bird-watch or swim.
Books are read and Brookies fried,
and the days pass like a dream.

But one evening campers collect on the shelf
of beach for a comic sight.
Blossom's been carried out of herself
by beams of pale moonlight.

Around the cabins she chases Alcott,
leaping a fallen log,
then through the shallows at awesome gait
she drives the astonished dog.

Her big bag bumps against her legs,
bounces and swings and sways.
Her tail flings into whirligigs
that would keep off flies for days.

Then Alcott collects himself and turns
and chases Blossom back,
then walks away as one who has learned
to take a more dignified tack.

Next all by herself she kicks up a melee.
Her udder shakes like a churn.
To watching campers it seems she really
intends to jump over the moon.

Then she chases the cook, who throws a broom
that flies between her horns,
and butts at the kitchen door for a home,
having forgotten barns.

Next morning the cow begins to moo.
The volume is astounding.
MOOOAWWW crosses the lake, and MAWWWW
from Whitecap comes rebounding.

Two cow moose in the lake lift heads,
their hides in sun like watered
silk, then scoot back into the woods,
their female nerves shattered.

MOOOAWWW! and in frightened blue and yellows
swallows and finches fly,
shaping in flocks like open umbrellas
wildly waved in the sky.

In boats the fisherman lash their poles
and catch themselves with their flies,
their timing spoiled by Blossom's bawls,
and trout refuse to rise.

MAWWOOOO! No one can think or read.
Such agony shakes the heart.
All morning Alcott hides in the woodshed.
At lunch, tempers are short.

A distant moo. Then silence. Some said
that boards were fitted in back
to hold her in, and Blossom was led
up a platform into the truck,

where she would bump and dip and soar
over many a rocky mile
to Greenville, which has a grocery store
as well as the nearest bull.

But the camp is worried. How many days
will the bellowing go on?
"I hope they leave her there," one says,
"until the heat is gone."

Birds criss-cross the sky with nowhere to go.
Suspense distorts the scene.
Alcott patrols on puzzled tiptoe.
It is late in the afternoon

when back she comes in the bumping truck
and steps down daintily,
a silent cow who refuses to look
anyone in the eye.

Nerves settle. A swarm of bumblebees
bends Blue-eyed grass for slaking.
A clink of pans from the kitchen says
the amorous undertaking

is happily concluded. Porches
hold pairs with books or drinks.
Resident squirrels resume their searches.
Alcott sits and thinks.

Beads of birds re-string themselves
along the telephone wire.
A young bull moose in velvet delves
in water near the shore.

Blossom lies like a crumpled sack
in blooms of chamomile.
Her gaze is inward. Her jaw is slack.
She might be said to smile.

At supper, laughter begins and ends,
for the mood is soft and shy.
One couple is seen to be holding hands
over wild raspberry pie.

Orange and gold flame Whitecap's peak
as the sun begins to set,
and anglers bend to the darkening lake
and bring up a flopping net.

When lamps go out and the moon lays light
on the lake like a great beachtowel,
Eros wings down to a fir to sit
and hoot* like a Long-eared owl.

* *The Long-eared owl's hoot resembles the whistle of tribute to the sight of something beautiful and sexy:* wheé whée-you"

MONA VAN DUYN

Mona Van Duyn (Mrs. Jarvis Thurston) was born in
Waterloo, Iowa in 1921 and since 1950 has lived in St.
Louis. She has taught at the University of Iowa
Writers' Workshop, the University of Louisville,
Washington University, The Salzburg Seminar in
American Studies and at Breadloaf and various other
writers' workshops around the United States. With
her husband she founded *Perspective, a Quarterly of
Literature* in 1947 and co-edited it until 1970. She has
received the Eunice Tietjens Award (1956) and the
Harriet Monroe Award (1968) from *Poetry*, the
Helen Bullis Prize (1964) from *Poetry Northwest*,
the National Book Award (1971) and (with Richard
Wilbur) The Bollingen Prize (1970). In 1976 she
received the Loines Prize from the National Institute
of Arts and Letters, and in 1980 was voted the $10,000
Fellowship of the Academy of American Poets. She
was one of the first five American poets to be given a
grant from the National Foundation for the Arts, and
held a Guggenheim Fellowship for 1972–1973. Wash-
ington University and Cornell College awarded her
the degree of Honorary Doctor of Letters.